A Child's First Library of Learning

The World We Live In

TIME-LIFE BOOKS • ALEXANDRIA, VIRGINIA

Contents

2

? Why Are Some Countries Hot While Others Are Cold?

ANSWER Places all over the world have different climates. That means they have their own regular weather patterns. The map below shows the earth's six climatic zones. Different plants and animals live in each zone. The way people live is different too.

▲ **Tropical.** Very hot, often rainy.

Equator

▲ **Temperate.** Excellent weather for farming.

▲ **Polar.** Always cold with snow and ice.

▲ **Dry.** Life can be very hard.

▲ **Highland.** Cold temperatures and windy.

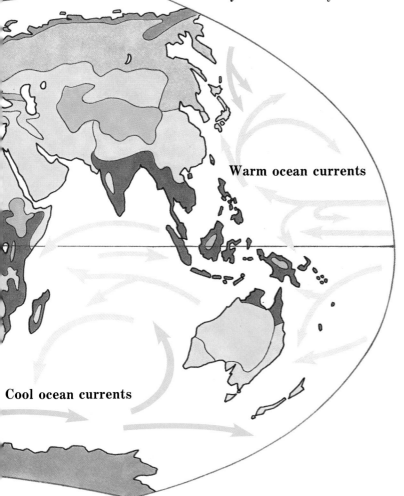

Warm ocean currents

Cool ocean currents

World climatic zones
■ Tropical

These areas near the equator are hot all year. Places with lots of rain have dense forests. Others with dry and rainy seasons have very tall grasses.

■ Temperate

These areas have changing weather with four clearly defined seasons. Because the climate is good, many people live in the temperate zones.

■ Dry

In this climatic zone there is almost no rain all year long. Areas with dry climates have deserts or steppes where different grasses grow.

■ Very cold

In this zone the summers are short and the winters are very harsh. The cold winter weather lasts for long periods of time.

■ Polar

Areas near the North and South Poles are covered by snow and ice most of the year. Polar areas are frozen the entire year.

■ Highland

Mountainous areas have this type of climate. The higher you go the colder it is, so higher ranges have the coldest weather.

● **To the Parent**

The main factor in the earth's climate is the amount of radiant energy received from the sun. Since the amount of radiation generally decreases as we go from the lower latitudes to the higher, climate varies according to latitude. Climate is also affected by altitude, ocean currents, wind, rain, topography and other conditions. Climate determines which plants and animals will flourish, and greatly influences diet, dress, housing, customs and culture. People everywhere have adapted their life styles to the climatic zones in which they live.

What Are the World's Hottest Places?

(ANSWER) In North Africa and the Arabian Peninsula there are deserts where very little rain falls. In this region temperatures even in the shade rise to 100° F. (38° C.) and sometimes can go as high as 120° F. (49° C.), about the same as a very hot bath. The sand and stones in direct sunlight are hot enough to burn you if you touch them.

▲ Massala, Iraq

■ The hottest day on earth

Al Aziziyah, Libya, September 3, 1922

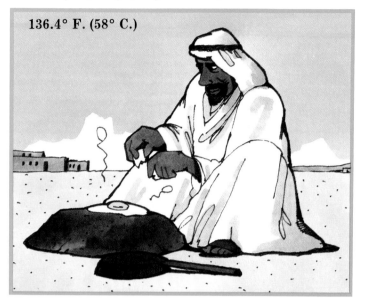

136.4° F. (58° C.)

■ Where it stays hot

In countries like Singapore, which are near the equator, the weather is hot all year.

● To the Parent

A dry desert climate extends from North Africa through the southwestern part of Asia. Temperatures frequently rise to between 100° F. (38° C.) and 120° F. (49° C.). The humidity is low, so perspiration evaporates rapidly. In such a climate people wear turbans on their heads and wrap their bodies in loose-fitting robes to protect themselves from the sun's fierce rays and against loss of moisture. People in these regions live in houses made of earth or brick to keep out the heat or in tents made of straw or animal skins.

How Do People Get Water in a Desert?

(ANSWER) Deserts have almost no rainfall but there is water. The water can be found deep in the ground. People in the desert must dig wells to reach this water. Or they must find special places where it has come to the surface. Such a place is called an oasis.

A traveler stops at an oasis. ▶

How does an oasis form?

Most water is deep below the desert. But sometimes the shape of the land changes. When water comes near the surface, a pool forms. Desert people often live near an oasis. They use it to water the land and grow food.

Rain

Desert

Oasis

Rainwater that has seeped into the ground

Rock that resists water

8

Drawing Water From a Desert Well

In a desert they dig into the ground until they reach underground water. A camel helps draw the water, which first goes to a reservoir and then is directed to ditches and used to water fields.

A slope is formed on the surface by digging.

The water is kept in a reservoir and channeled into ditches to be used for irrigating farmland.

What is a kanat?

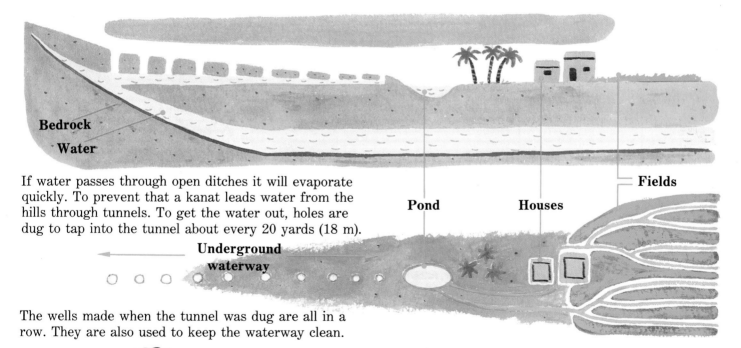

Bedrock

Water

If water passes through open ditches it will evaporate quickly. To prevent that a kanat leads water from the hills through tunnels. To get the water out, holes are dug to tap into the tunnel about every 20 yards (18 m).

Underground waterway

Pond

Houses

Fields

The wells made when the tunnel was dug are all in a row. They are also used to keep the waterway clean.

● **To the Parent**

In a desert there is little rainfall, but water that has fallen in another area will flow underground to surface later as a spring. Wells may also be dug to get at the underground water. The kanat irrigation system is found in West and Central Asia. Ancient records reveal that it has been used since the 6th Century B.C. In some desert regions very large irrigation projects have been undertaken to build dams and provide water, which the people living in these areas use to cultivate date palms, wheat, barley and other grains.

? Why Are There So Many Camels In Desert Countries?

(ANSWER) In the desert it is hard to find food and water. People and most animals find it hard to survive. But the camel is born to live in the desert. It can survive in the harsh desert climate, and it can help people live there too.

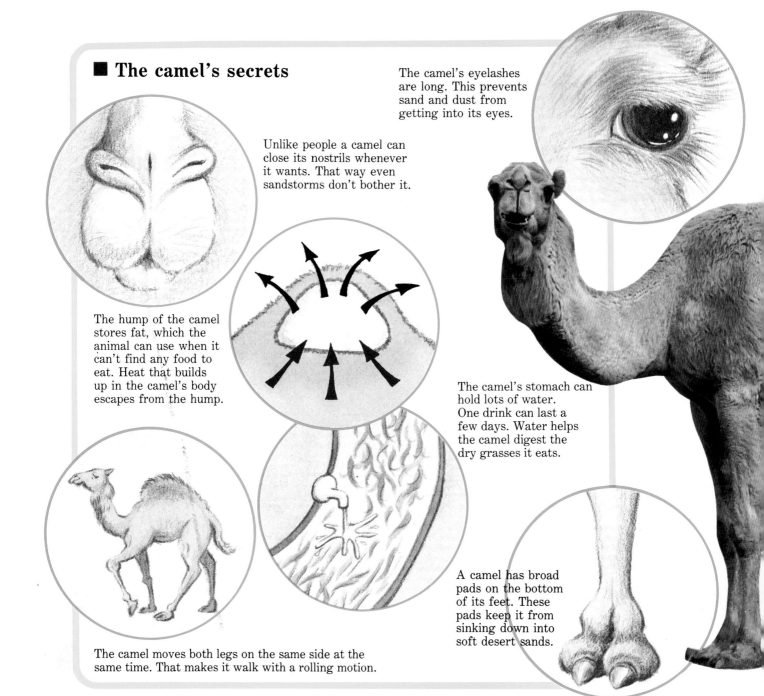

■ The camel's secrets

The camel's eyelashes are long. This prevents sand and dust from getting into its eyes.

Unlike people a camel can close its nostrils whenever it wants. That way even sandstorms don't bother it.

The hump of the camel stores fat, which the animal can use when it can't find any food to eat. Heat that builds up in the camel's body escapes from the hump.

The camel's stomach can hold lots of water. One drink can last a few days. Water helps the camel digest the dry grasses it eats.

A camel has broad pads on the bottom of its feet. These pads keep it from sinking down into soft desert sands.

The camel moves both legs on the same side at the same time. That makes it walk with a rolling motion.

■ The ship of the desert

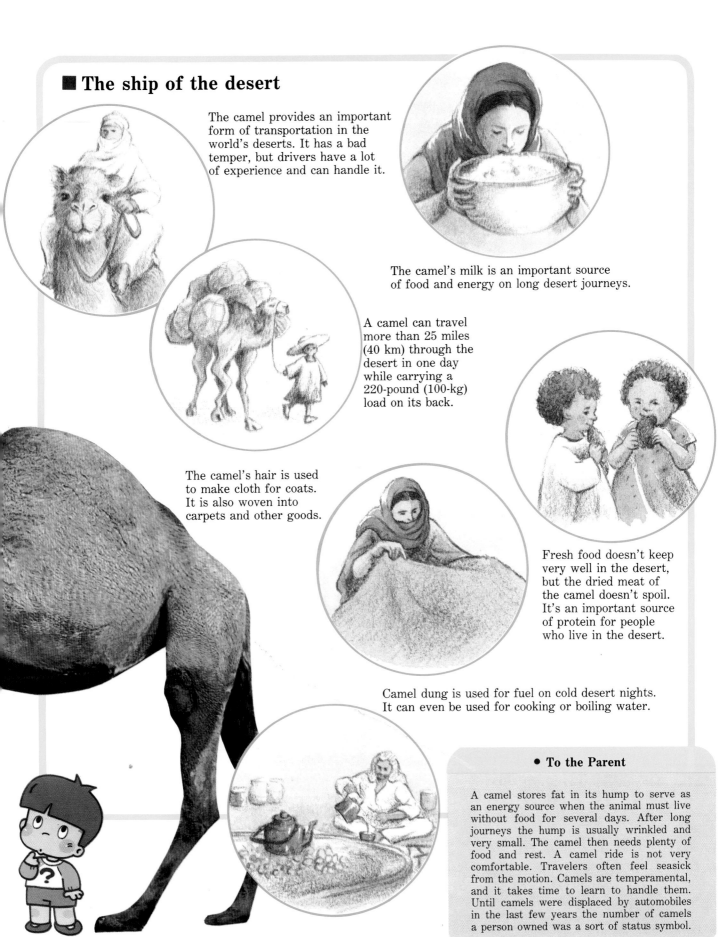

The camel provides an important form of transportation in the world's deserts. It has a bad temper, but drivers have a lot of experience and can handle it.

The camel's milk is an important source of food and energy on long desert journeys.

A camel can travel more than 25 miles (40 km) through the desert in one day while carrying a 220-pound (100-kg) load on its back.

The camel's hair is used to make cloth for coats. It is also woven into carpets and other goods.

Fresh food doesn't keep very well in the desert, but the dried meat of the camel doesn't spoil. It's an important source of protein for people who live in the desert.

Camel dung is used for fuel on cold desert nights. It can even be used for cooking or boiling water.

● To the Parent

A camel stores fat in its hump to serve as an energy source when the animal must live without food for several days. After long journeys the hump is usually wrinkled and very small. The camel then needs plenty of food and rest. A camel ride is not very comfortable. Travelers often feel seasick from the motion. Camels are temperamental, and it takes time to learn to handle them. Until camels were displaced by automobiles in the last few years the number of camels a person owned was a sort of status symbol.

❓ Did You Know That Some People Build Houses High in the Air?

(ANSWER) One place that this is true is the country of New Guinea. In the jungle there it rains a lot. The air near the ground is hot and muggy, so people build houses in trees or above water. In that way they can feel the breeze and stay cooler. Of course you will not find many houses like this in the cities

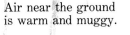

Air near the ground is warm and muggy.

There are so many trees and bushes in some parts of the tropics that less sunlight reaches the ground than elsewhere.

There's danger in some places from harmful insects and wild animals.

■ A tree house

A tree is a good place for a house in parts of the tropics. Higher up the breeze makes it cooler. It's sunnier too, and that helps keep some insects away.

■ House on stilts

On the coast of Papua New Guinea, which is near Australia, houses are often built over the water. They are held up by a framework of stilts. Such houses get more breeze and are cooler. Most of the people who live in places like this travel around by boat.

▲ This house on the coast of New Guinea is built over water.

A long house in Borneo

On the island of Borneo houses have raised floors and may be more than 50 feet (15 m) long. Several families live in separate rooms in these houses.

▼ Domestic animals are kept under the house.

▲ This long house was built in the middle of the jungle.

▲ People are safe from heavy rains and floods.

● To the Parent

Houses everywhere are built according to conditions in regional topography and climate. In tropical areas houses have raised floors to improve circulation of air and counter the effect of heat and humidity. Houses in trees provide protection against insects and animals, and those over water give easy access to waterways used for transport. The Borneo long house is like a village, with several families living under one communal roof.

? How Do People Live In the Amazon Jungle?

ANSWER The famous Amazon River is in South America. It is 4,000 miles (6,400 km) long. The land around the river is covered by hot, dense jungles. The people living in the jungles along the Amazon don't wear much clothing. They hunt, gather and prepare their food much the same way their ancestors did. The way of life in the Amazon jungles hasn't changed very much in thousands of years.

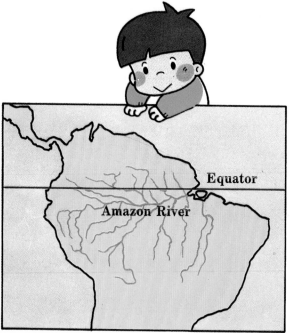

The life of the people of the Amazon

They weave straw into a kind of cloth with which they make hammocks and other things.

They put a stick of sugar cane into a post and twist it to squeeze out the juice.

They put overripe bananas into a wooden trough and crush them to get banana juice.

■ What do these people eat?

People living in these jungles must grow food. First they clear jungle land by burning it. Then they grow cassava, bananas, papaya and sugar cane. Cassava is a starchy root used as food in tropical countries.

Tapir

Anteater

Jaguar

Howler monkey

Piranha

Papaya

Catfish

How do they eat cassava?

First they remove the skin from cassava root and wash the root well.

They grate the root to separate the starch, and then they bake the starch.

It is very humid in the jungle, so people sleep in hammocks. At night they light fires to keep warm and to keep insects and animals away while they sleep.

● **To the Parent**

The Amazon River basin has huge areas of tropical rain forest and jungle. Among the inhabitants of this region are Indian tribes whose way of life has not changed for thousands of years. Because of the high temperature and humidity they wear little or no clothing. These Indians hunt animals with poison arrows and spears and farm land reclaimed from the jungle by the slash-and-burn method.

What Is the Coldest Place Where People Live?

ANSWER The arctic region is covered with snow and ice for almost the whole year. The temperature in the middle of the winter can go down to –60° F. (–51° C.). When it gets this cold frost forms on eyebrows and eyelashes. It is colder than inside a freezer.

■ Warm clothes to wear

Clothes made of animal skins

Reindeer hide parka

Fur-lined mittens

Trousers made of polar bear skin

Fur-lined boots

Shoes made of sealskin

When it's very cold clothes like those on the left are worn under the parka and boots on the right.

■ What was the coldest day?

On July 21, 1983, at
the Vostok station
in Antarctica
the thermometer
dropped to
-128.6° F.
(-89.2° C.).
That is the
coldest day
on record.

■ Winters are warmer in London

The average winter
temperature in London
is 40° F. (4° C.).

● **To the Parent**

Ice and snow cover Greenland and the tundra of Canada
and Alaska most of the year. The Eskimos who live in
those regions wear multiple layers of coats, trousers
and boots made of animal skins for protection against
the extreme cold. They live in earthen houses, in
structures built of blocks of snow and ice or in tents
made from animal skins. In this way people are able
to survive even in bitterly cold parts of the world.

Why Do the Lapps Keep Herds of Reindeer?

(ANSWER) The Lapps are people who live in the northern part of Europe where it is very cold. They depend on the reindeer for much of what they need to survive. As the reindeer travel in search of food, many Lapps travel with them.

How do they use the reindeer?

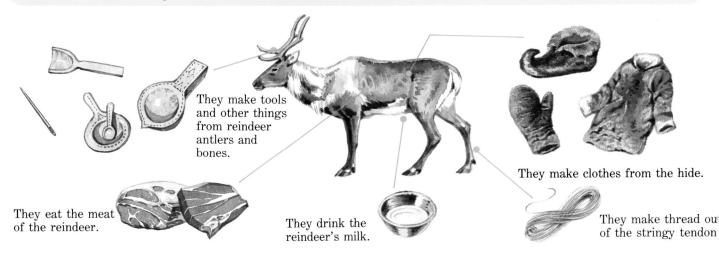

They make tools and other things from reindeer antlers and bones.

They eat the meat of the reindeer.

They drink the reindeer's milk.

They make clothes from the hide.

They make thread out of the stringy tendon

The Life of the Lapps

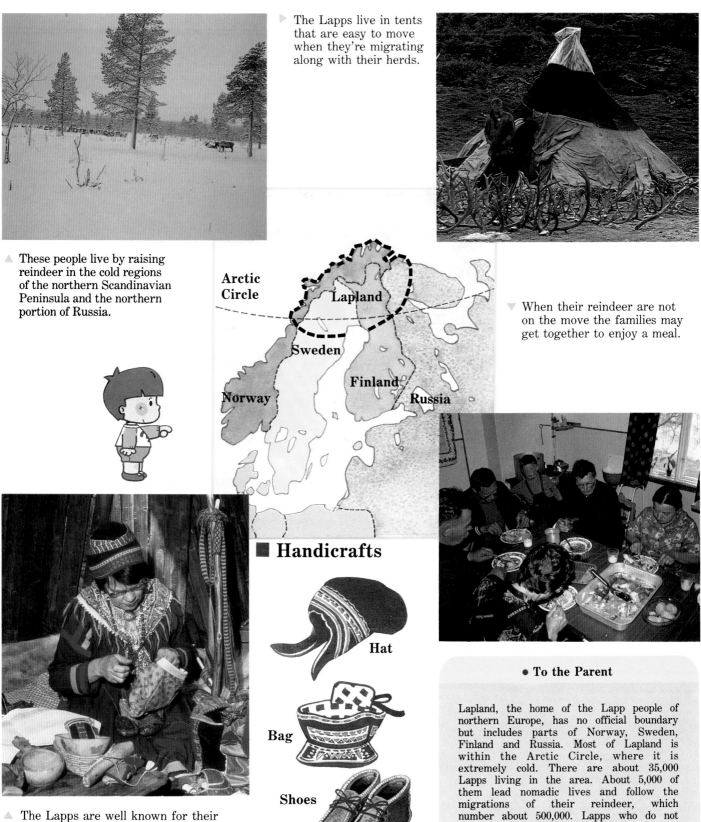

The Lapps live in tents that are easy to move when they're migrating along with their herds.

These people live by raising reindeer in the cold regions of the northern Scandinavian Peninsula and the northern portion of Russia.

Arctic Circle

Lapland

Sweden

Finland

Norway

Russia

When their reindeer are not on the move the families may get together to enjoy a meal.

■ Handicrafts

Hat

Bag

Shoes

The Lapps are well known for their distinctive handicrafts and costumes. Their work can be seen in markets or sometimes at outdoor museums.

● To the Parent

Lapland, the home of the Lapp people of northern Europe, has no official boundary but includes parts of Norway, Sweden, Finland and Russia. Most of Lapland is within the Arctic Circle, where it is extremely cold. There are about 35,000 Lapps living in the area. About 5,000 of them lead nomadic lives and follow the migrations of their reindeer, which number about 500,000. Lapps who do not herd reindeer usually make their living by fishing, farming or forestry.

What Is Life Like For Eskimos of the Far North?

ANSWER The areas where Eskimos live are covered by snow and ice most of the year. When they hunt in cold weather they wear clothes made out of caribou hide and sealskin. In the past Eskimos were nomads who lived in igloos made of snow in winter and tents in summer. Now most live in one place all year.

▼ An Eskimo hunts caribou, a typical game animal.

The Eskimo diet

Much of Alaska is covered with snow and ice. That means that it is hard to get fresh vegetables. The Eskimos include raw meat in their diet so that they can get enough vitamins.

■ What animals do Eskimos hunt?

When Eskimos kill animals they use the meat for food, the fat for fuel and the hide for clothes.

◁ **Whale**

Walrus ▽

▲ **Seal**

▽ **Salmon**

▲ **Hare**

Duck ▷

Ptarmigan ▷

In the past the Eskimo people didn't eat starch or sugar. Because of that they didn't get many cavities in their teeth. But in recent years their eating habits have changed, and cavities are more common today.

What Do the People Do?

The Eskimos have developed special skills in their everyday lives to help them survive under extremely harsh natural conditions.

▷ This Eskimo native prepares a freshly caught fish for eating. Almost any place can be used as a kitchen in the arctic wilderness.

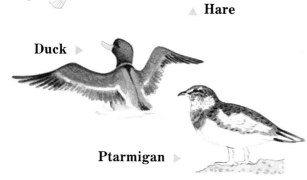

◁ Since Alaska's winter is very long, Eskimos enjoy the sunshine they get during the short summer.

● To the Parent

Eskimos live in Greenland, Canada and Alaska, with a small number in Siberia. The total population is about 90,000, about one third of whom live in Alaska. Most of them still hunt caribou in the interior of Alaska and seals, salmon and whales along the coast. Some Eskimos still move each season, building igloos from snow in winter and living in tents of caribou skins during the summer. In some areas strawberries or celery are grown in summer, but raw meat is still the Eskimo's best source of needed vitamins. The word Eskimo means eater of raw meat in one of the native Alaskan dialects, and recently the name Inuit has come to be preferred instead of Eskimo. As the Eskimo life style undergoes change, more and more are moving into towns.

❓ How Do Eskimos Build Snow Igloos?

ANSWER Snow igloos are made by cutting hard-packed snow into blocks and stacking blocks on each other to form sort of an upside-down bowl.

Today not many Eskimos live in these houses of snow. Most of them build houses of wood or stone to keep them warm during the cold weather.

▲ Eskimos work in bitter cold to build their snow houses.

Five steps to an igloo

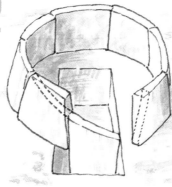

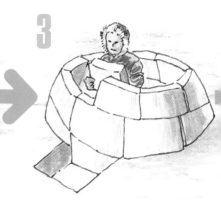

First the hard-packed snow is cut into evenly shaped blocks.

Next the blocks are cut at an angle to fit side by side in a circle.

Then the blocks are built up in a circle until only one space remains.

Isn't It Cold in a House Made of Snow?

If you touch the walls of an igloo they feel cold, but they keep out the wind and snow. The inside of the house is kept warm by burning oil made from seal fat. Furs are laid on a raised part of the floor so people can sit down without feeling cold. It's so warm inside that babies can sleep naked in fur beds and feather quilts.

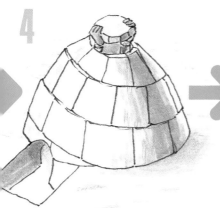

Finally the last block is fitted into place at the top of the igloo.

A hole is made to let the smoke out, and a wooden or fur door is attached.

● **To the Parent**

Only the Canadian Eskimo has traditionally lived in snow houses. The snow igloo described here is used in winter, usually when people are on the move during the hunt. A snow igloo about 12 feet (3.5 m) or so in diameter is large enough to hold five or six people easily and can be built by one person in a little more than two hours. The dome-shaped dwelling is so sturdy that children can even play on the top of it. The igloo is warmed by the burning of seal oil or other animal oil. As the snow melts along the walls any gaps are sealed so that heat cannot escape. Most Canadian Eskimos live in the tundra. Temperatures never exceed 50° F. (10° C.) even in summer and may go as low as −22° F. (−30° C.) in the winter.

How Do the People of Korea Keep Their Houses Warm?

ANSWER A fire is built under a large cast-iron pot in the kitchen. Heat from the fire passes under the floor to warm the room. Stones and dirt are laid under the floor to help keep the temperature at a comfortable level. This system is called an ondol. Sometimes smoke and gas from the fire enter the home and make people ill.

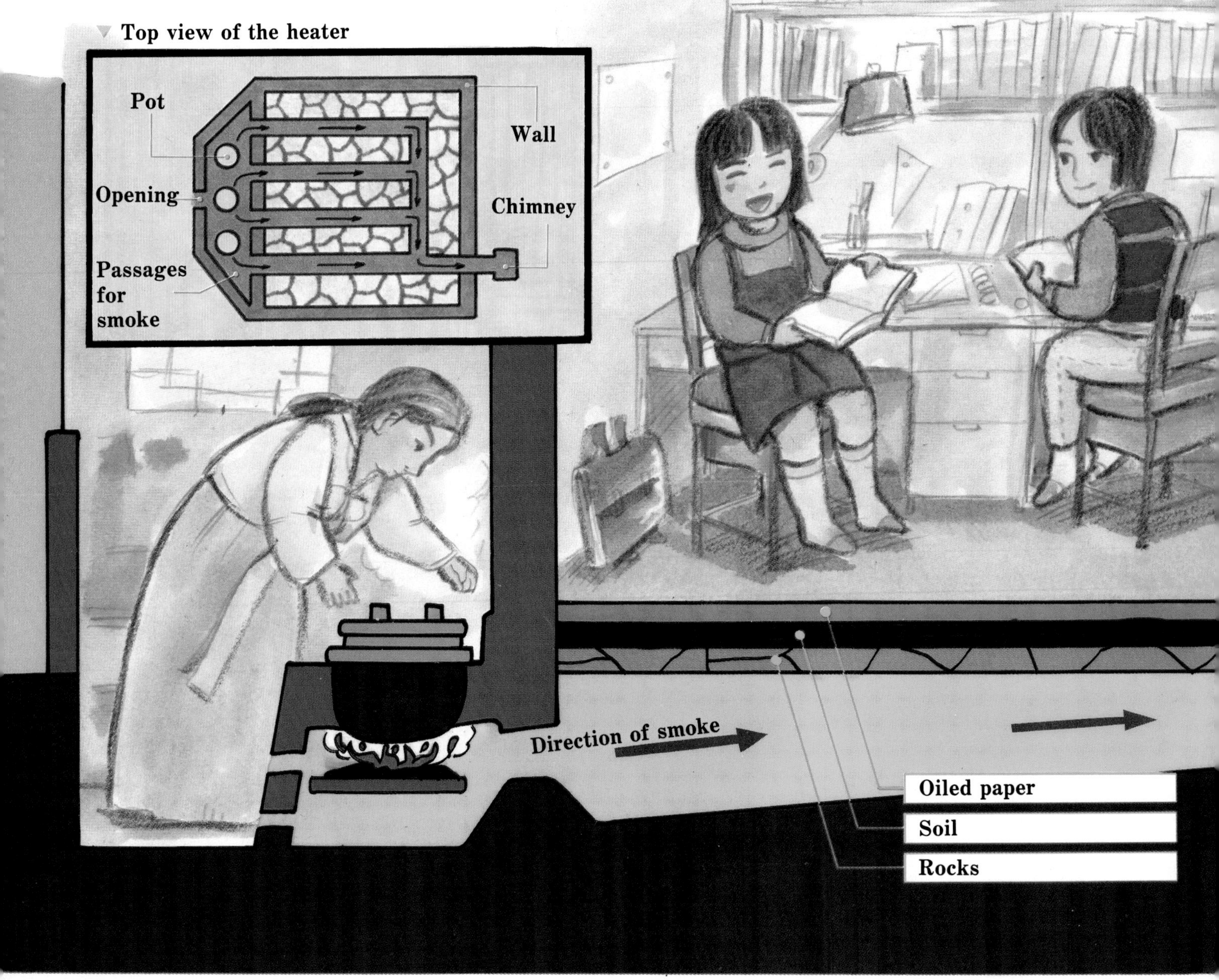

▼ **Top view of the heater**

Pot

Opening

Passages for smoke

Wall

Chimney

Direction of smoke

Oiled paper

Soil

Rocks

The chimney lets smoke escape and also is an important decoration for the house.

Other Kinds of Heaters

People heat their homes to keep warm and comfortable. They use wood, charcoal, coal, heating oil, gas, electricity or other fuels.

Open hearth ▷

Fireplace ▽

Coal stove

Gas heater

Table heater ▲

Steam radiator ◁

● To the Parent

Korean homes traditionally have been one-storied due to the ondol system of heating through the floor. For maximum heat efficiency ceilings tend to be low. The rooms are small and have small windows. Wallpaper is also used to hold in heat. In homes with an ondol the bedding usually is bright and decorative because during the daytime it is put out close to the flue to dry out.

What Is a Yurt And How Is It Built?

ANSWER People who move from place to place are called nomads. In the country of Mongolia many nomads raise sheep. They move to find fresh pastures for their sheep. Because they move a lot the Mongols need houses that are easy to carry with them. Yurts are like tents. They can be taken down and put up again easily. They are made of soft cloth that comes from the sheep's wool. The cloth is laid over a wooden frame. The yurt's shape keeps it standing firmly against strong winds, which pass right over the rounded top.

How they put it up

Nomads move to as many as 20 new pastures in one year. That's why the yurt is made so it can be taken apart quickly. The frame, the felt and even the carpets that are put on the ground to serve as a floor are easy to pack.

Once they are taken down yurts are put on camels or wagons.

After finding a new site everyone puts up the yurt.

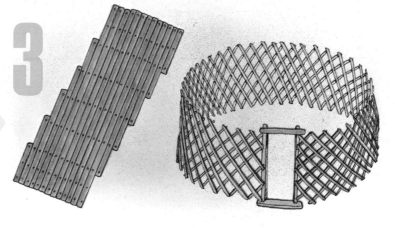

The framework is unrolled and the whole thing is tied up with cords.

What's a Yurt Like Inside?

The inside of a yurt forms a single large room. There are beds, cooking utensils and other household items, with a stove in the center of the typical yurt. The floor is covered with carpets, and there's a place for each member of the nomad family to sit.

▲ Nomads in Inner Mongolia raise sheep like these.

5 Felt is laid over the yurt. The cloth that covers the hole on top is tied with thongs.

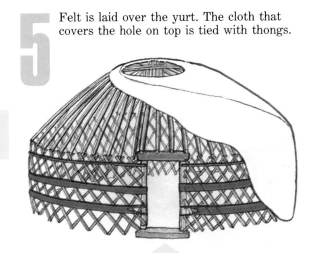

4

The entrance always faces toward the south for warmth.

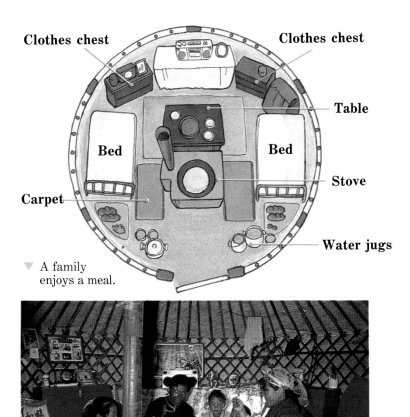

Clothes chest

Clothes chest

Table

Bed

Bed

Stove

Carpet

Water jugs

▼ A family enjoys a meal.

● **To the Parent**

The steppes that stretch from Mongolia through Central Asia are inhabited by nomadic people who follow their flocks. These nomads are on the move all year round in search of pastureland. Their houses, called yurts, can be moved easily in a wagon or on a camel's back. Usually a yurt can be put up in about 30 minutes. When it is taken down and packed it weighs about 550 pounds (250 kg). The yurt's construction begins with a framework of willow branches. Sheets of felt made of pressed wool are laid over the framework, then waterproof cloth is used to cover the layer of felt. The result is a sturdy shelter.

27

Why Do the People of the Netherlands Build So Many Dikes?

ANSWER The Netherlands is a small country of low, flat land. To make their country bigger the Dutch reclaimed land from the sea. They did this by building dikes along the shore. These great walls of dirt prevent floods by holding back the sea water.

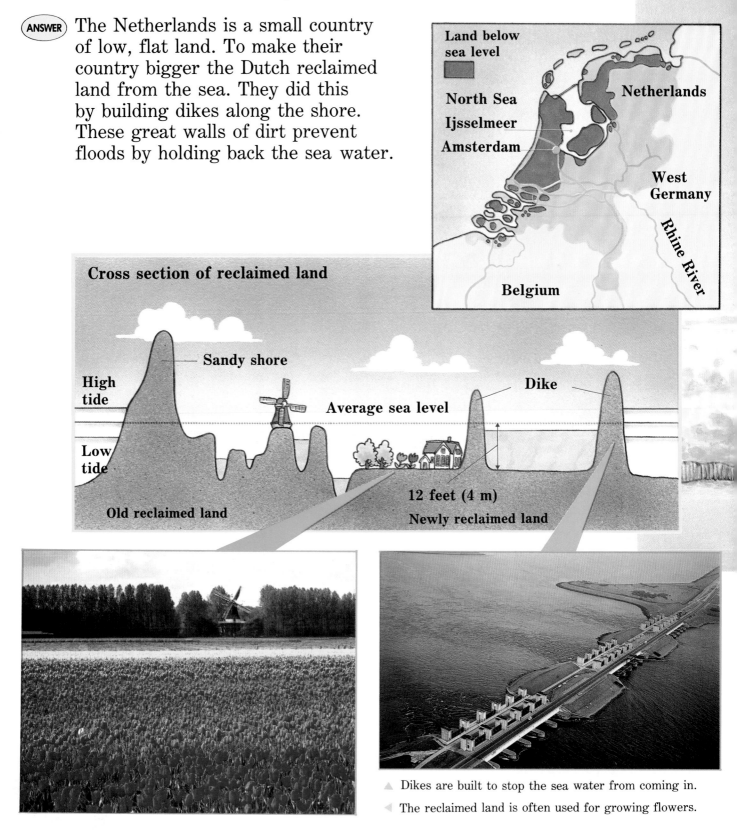

Land below sea level

North Sea

Ijsselmeer

Amsterdam

Netherlands

West Germany

Rhine River

Belgium

Cross section of reclaimed land

Sandy shore

High tide

Low tide

Average sea level

Dike

12 feet (4 m)

Old reclaimed land

Newly reclaimed land

△ Dikes are built to stop the sea water from coming in.

◁ The reclaimed land is often used for growing flowers.

Why Do They Have So Many Windmills?

The windmills harness the energy of the wind so that water can be pumped up out of the country's low-lying areas and into the canals that run through the countryside. Because it's very important to be able to pump out as much water as possible, there are rows and rows of windmills lined up in the Netherlands' fields.

Windmills are used to pump water from low-lying land.

They once were used for grinding grain too.

Wearing wooden shoes

The wooden shoes, or sabots, that the Dutch wear are made of beech, chestnut or other woods that resist water. Water does not hurt them, so they're good for walking in the wetlands.

● **To the Parent**

Because much of the Netherlands is at sea level or lower, the country has been threatened by floods throughout its history. Starting many years ago dikes were built at the mouths of rivers to help prevent floods. Pumps powered by windmills were used in the effort to reclaim the flats along the seashore and deltas so that the country would have more land. Many of these areas, called polders, were reclaimed in the first half of the 17th Century to be used for agriculture. Electric pumps are now used to maintain them.

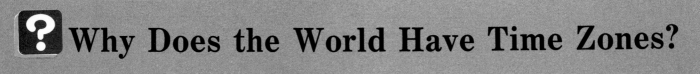

Why Does the World Have Time Zones?

ANSWER The earth turns around every 24 hours. As the world spins, different parts of it face the sun's light. So that our daytime hours will occur when it is light, the world is divided into 24 time zones.

London

Moscow

New Delhi

Tokyo

International date line

This map shows some times around the world. When children in the United States are waking up or are in school it is midnight in Tokyo, Japan. What are you doing while the Japanese children are in school?

San Francisco

At sea

Rio de Janeiro

On a sunny day, find a tree or pole stuck in the ground. Place a small stone at the tip of its shadow. Come back an hour later and place a stone where the shadow now falls. Do this for several hours, marking each new spot. What have you observed?

● **To the Parent**

The earth rotates on its axis once every 24 hours, moving through 15 degrees of longitude every hour. For this reason there is a time difference of one hour for every 15 degrees of longitude. Time zones, each with a width of approximately 15 degrees of longitude, have been drawn around the world, with slight deviations allowed for political boundaries or geographical features. Standard time for any location is calculated according to its distance east or west of 0° longitude, or the prime meridian, which runs through Greenwich, England. Times around the world are stated in terms of Greenwich mean time plus or minus a number of hours. Chicago, for instance, is GMT −6 hours. The calendar day begins at the international date line, which corresponds approximately to the 180th meridian.

31

❓ Why Do People in Various Lands Use Different Kinds of Greetings?

ANSWER When you see someone you greet him by saying "Hello." You may also shake that person's hand or wave to him. These are some of the ways you show friendliness or respect. In other countries people use their own words and signals to greet and say hello to each other. Although the greetings and actions are different the feeling is the same.

Hello

Konnichiwa

Namaste

▲ In Japan people kneel on the floor and bow their head deeply. If they are outside and standing they might bow several times.

▲ In India people place their hands together as some of us do when we are saying a prayer. This is their way to greet people and also to express thanks. It would be very impolite not to do this.

◄ The Maoris, the native people of New Zealand, greet each other by sticking out their tongues.

▲ In Russia as well as in other Slavic countries, friends show how happy they are when they meet by rubbing their faces cheek to cheek. They probably would not do that when meeting strangers.

▼ When people in Arab countries who are close friends meet they usually greet each other by touching the tips of their noses together. That is not strange to them.

● To the Parent

Greetings are an essential part of everyday life. From "Good morning" at the start of the day to "Good night" at bedtime we use various phrases for greetings and farewells, as the occasion demands. Greetings often consist not only of words but accompanying postures or gestures, sometimes called body language. These differ from country to country and are of a wide variety, including bowing, shaking hands and pressing the hands together. But they are similar in that they show friendliness and respect and are taught to children in all societies to promote smooth relationships.

How Do People Say "Thank You"?

People who speak different languages have their own way of saying thanks.

Thank you very much.

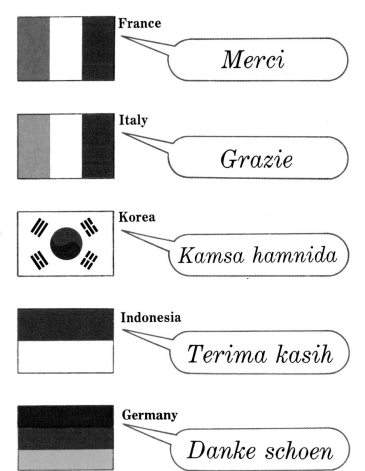

France

Merci

Italy

Grazie

Korea

Kamsa hamnida

Indonesia

Terima kasih

Germany

Danke schoen

33

When Did People Start Shaking Hands?

(ANSWER) No one knows exactly when it got started, but the popular custom of touching or holding hands has a long history. Many people around the world now are in the habit of shaking hands when they meet or say goodbye.

▶ Showing the hands palms up meant a person wanted peace.

▼ In ancient Greece extending the hands with palms together showed friendship.

Power

▲ In very ancient times the hand was used in signs of strength or power.

▶ When Arabs meet one another it is their tradition to place their hands together. This is their way of showing modesty.

▶ The ancient Greeks extended the right hand to friends.

When Did the Custom of Kissing Start?

Kissing was practiced in ancient times to show respect for those above you. In ancient Rome the people of the upper class greeted each other with a kiss on the mouth or eye. But nowadays kissing on the lips or cheek is a sign of love and trust between family members, friends and couples. At a wedding the kiss is a special symbol of the bond between husband and wife.

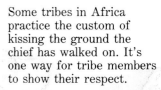
Some tribes in Africa practice the custom of kissing the ground the chief has walked on. It's one way for tribe members to show their respect.

In some countries people kiss their partner after a dance.

■ Kissing to show love

No one knows exactly when the custom started, but kissing as an expression of affection or love goes back to olden times. In most cultures it seems only natural for parents to kiss their young children, and in many countries they will continue to kiss and hug them even as adults.

Smack!

? Why Are There So Many Different Kinds of Writing?

ANSWER People have been speaking in different languages for thousands of years. The language a person speaks depends on where he lives. People have also developed their own ways of writing. Today there are about 3,000 different languages spoken around the world.

▲ **Signs in Greece**

▼ In China people use characters that have meaning just as words do. This man is writing with a brush, but the characters can also be written with a pen or pencil.

▲ **A world of books:** 1. Kampuchea 2. Laos 3. Nepal 4. Sri Lanka 5. Pakistan

When was writing first used?

People first started writing about 5,000 years ago. They wrote in the country of Egypt and in Mesopotamia, which was part of what is now Iraq.

▷ **Cuneiform characters**
This system of writing uses characters shaped like wedges and got its name from the Latin word cuneus, meaning wedge.

6. Russia 7. South Korea 8. Bangladesh
9. Japan 10. United States 11. China 12. Iraq

Writing numbers

There are also different systems of numerals used to write numbers. Arabic numerals are the most common. These originated in India but got their name because Arabs took them to the West.

▽ Western style	▽ Arabian style	▽ Chinese numerals	▽ Roman numerals
1	١	一	I
2	٢	二	II
3	٣	三	III
4	٤	四	IV
5	٥	五	V

❓ Why Do People Around the World Dress Differently?

ANSWER People dress the way they do for several reasons. Their clothing must suit the weather where they live. In many places it must be made from materials that people can easily find around them. Every place has its own customs which also help decide what we wear.

▶ This is a costume that men in Austria have worn for ages.

▼ The clothes worn by this Dutch girl include a hat and wooden shoes that are like the ones the Dutch have always liked.

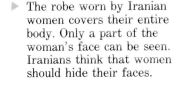

▲ These are the costumes that Spanish men and women wear when they perform the lively dance called the flamenco.

▶ The robe worn by Iranian women covers their entire body. Only a part of the woman's face can be seen. Iranians think that women should hide their faces.

▲ The clothing worn by a man in the city of Marrakech, Morocco, consists of a long, gownlike garment as well as a type of hat that is called a fez. Morocco is in Africa.

These are some of the costumes worn in the Ukraine.

Japanese men and women frequently wear kimonos during the New Year season. Traditional kimonos are also worn by Japanese people on other formal occasions such as weddings, funerals and festivals.

This is a favorite dress of Bavaria in Germany. The man is wearing a type of short embroidered trousers.

This Mexican man's hat is called a sombrero. The blanket he drapes across his shoulder is known as a serape.

The clothing of an Inca woman in South America's Andes Mountains includes many layers of skirts to keep her warm.

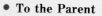

● **To the Parent**

Various kinds of ethnic costumes are worn in different parts of the world. Factors such as religion, esthetic perceptions and climatic conditions all influence regional styles of dress. Clothing was originally extremely basic and was designed primarily for protection against intemperate weather. As civilization developed, clothing began to include a decorative function, which eventually assumed primary importance. Gender and social class also helped determine the way in which people dressed. Other factors that affected the development of clothing styles were the influence of other cultures or invasion of a community or nation by another with a different culture.

 Why Do the Scots Wear Kilts?

(ANSWER) In ancient times the people living in Scotland wrapped their body in a checkered cloth called a tartan. It was hard to work when wearing a tartan, so they took off the part covering the upper part of the body. Only the portion on the lower body was kept. The modern kilt is only half the original.

■ Various clans' tartans

Kilts are made from a tartan, a checkered cloth. Each family, or clan, has its own pattern.

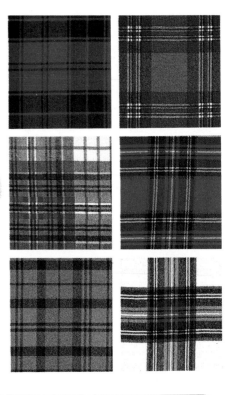

The kilt had no pockets, so people carried a special kind of pouch. In formal dress they wore one pouch in the day and a different one in the evening.

Leather: day   **Fur: night**

Kilt pins are used to fasten the kilt so it won't come open. These may have precious stones on them when they are worn at formal affairs in the evening.

For day

For night

For night   **Day or night**

Because soldiers once wore kilts, men wearing a kilt often place a knife in the stocking on the side on which a sword would be carried.

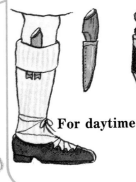

For daytime

For nighttime

When Are Kilts Worn?

The kilt is now what the men in Scotland wear on formal occasions.
It is usually worn on New Year's Day, to church and to weddings and
graduation ceremonies. In the past the kilt, though different in
form, was an everyday garment, and it was worn on the battlefield.

What Are Bagpipes?

The bagpipe is a musical instrument
which is famous for the unusual
sounds that it makes. It is popular
in Scotland. In Scottish regiments
of the British army, soldiers play
music on bagpipes. The other
soldiers march along to the music.

Air comes in
by a tube.

Drone

This drone is
essential for
playing low notes.

Bag

Scottish bagpipes are
named for the bag that
is used to hold air.

Chanter

This plays the melody.

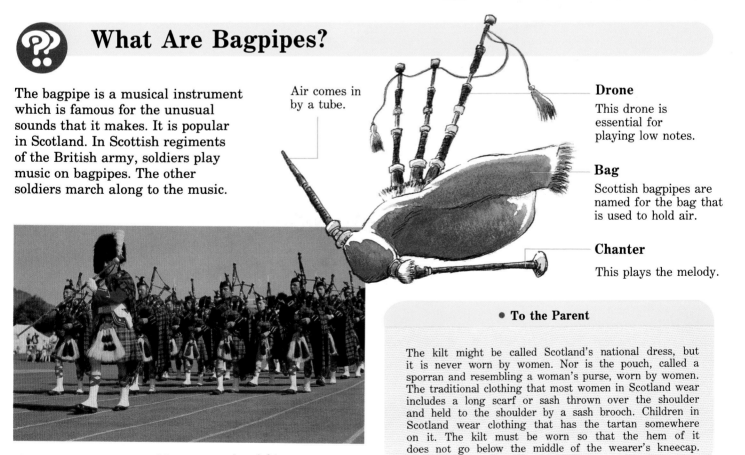

▲ A regimental pipe band is a spectacular sight.

● **To the Parent**

The kilt might be called Scotland's national dress, but
it is never worn by women. Nor is the pouch, called a
sporran and resembling a woman's purse, worn by women.
The traditional clothing that most women in Scotland wear
includes a long scarf or sash thrown over the shoulder
and held to the shoulder by a sash brooch. Children in
Scotland wear clothing that has the tartan somewhere
on it. The kilt must be worn so that the hem of it
does not go below the middle of the wearer's kneecap.

 What Is a Sari?

ANSWER A sari is a traditional dress worn by Indian women. But it is just a large piece of cloth. Before putting on a sari the woman puts on a sari blouse and a slip. Then she takes the cloth, which is extremely long, and wraps, folds and tucks it around herself.

The sari is from 3 to 4 feet (90 to 120 cm) wide and from 13 to 36 feet (4 to 11 m) long.

An Indian woman wearing a sari

Step by step

1
Tuck one end of the sari into the top of the slip and wrap it around once.

2
Wrap it around again, leaving a loop on one side. Fold the end into pleats.

3
Carefully drape the pleated end across the left shoulder.

Do You Know What a Dhoti Is?

A dhoti is a long loincloth worn by Hindu men in India and other countries. Like a sari it is a single piece of cloth.

To put on a dhoti

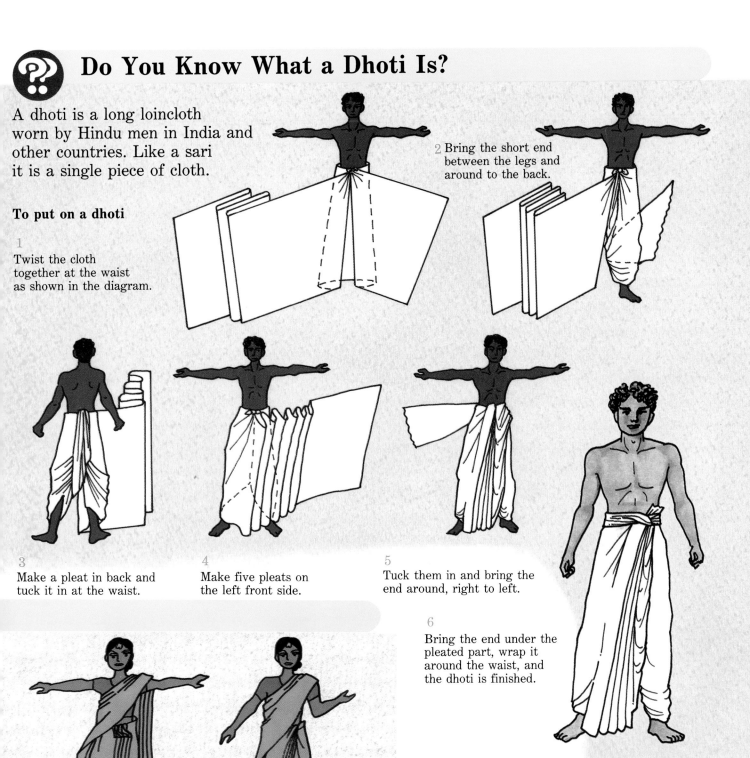

1

Twist the cloth together at the waist as shown in the diagram.

2 Bring the short end between the legs and around to the back.

3
Make a pleat in back and tuck it in at the waist.

4
Make five pleats on the left front side.

5
Tuck them in and bring the end around, right to left.

6
Bring the end under the pleated part, wrap it around the waist, and the dhoti is finished.

4
In the center front, pleat the rest of the cloth.

5
Tuck the pleats in at the waist and you're finished.

● **To the Parent**

The sari is worn in various ways. The one illustrated here is known as the National Style. In other styles the end of the sari may be draped over the head or passed over the right shoulder to conceal the blouse. This shows the versatility with which a single length of cloth serves as a garment. The dhoti also is one piece of cloth. It can be worn in the manner shown here or can be simply wrapped around the waist. Such garments are the product of climate and social custom, and combine function with an attractive appearance.

? Why Do People in India Eat Spicy Curry?

(ANSWER) In India people eat lots of curry. This mixture of spices makes their food taste very hot. People in India like curry. And the spices they put into it help them in many ways.

■ A dish for a hot climate

1 It gives people a good appetite.

2 It helps to digest food.

3 It kills germs.

44

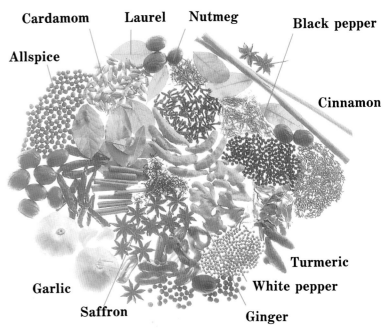

■ About spices

Spices come from seeds and leaves.
Have you tasted any of these spices?

Cardamom **Laurel** **Nutmeg**

Allspice **Black pepper**

Cinnamon

Turmeric

Garlic **White pepper**

Saffron **Ginger**

It keeps people cool by making them sweat.

? Why Do So Many People Eat Rice?

ANSWER Grains are an important source of food in most countries. The most common grains are rice, wheat and corn. Rice is grown in many countries of the world but mostly in Asia. Since so much rice is grown in Asia, more of it is eaten there than anywhere else.

Japan
Plain white rice is almost always eaten with traditional Japanese meals.

France
A sweet made of rice and milk is popular in France.

Vietnam
Vietnamese people eat white rice with many kinds of food.

Syria

Rice is cooked with lamb or chicken and is served on a large platter.

United States

Rice sometimes replaces potatoes as a vegetable on an American dinner plate.

Spain

Rice with vegetables and seafood makes a popular dish called paella.

People all over the world eat rice, but they prepare it in different ways.

● **To the Parent**

Rice is eaten in approximately 130 countries, with the highest per capita consumption in China, Indonesia and Bangladesh. More than 90% of the world's rice is grown in Asia, where it is a staple food. A distinctive feature of a people and culture is the way they prepare and eat rice, which may be steamed, boiled or fried.

What Musical Instruments Do Different Peoples Play?

ANSWER People everywhere like music. That's why there are so many different kinds of instruments. There are three basic ways that instruments make music. You bang or strike some like a drum. You pluck or strum the strings on others. And there are still other instruments which you blow air into to make a pleasing sound.

Instruments that you strike

Percussion board ▶
A wooden board is struck with a stick. Even a shield can become a musical instrument.

◀ **Tabla**
These drums are used in north India. They have high tones and low tones.

Krotala ▼
This instrument was used in ancient Egypt, Greece and Rome. The disks at the end are very much like cymbals.

Steel drum ▶
This instrument is from Trinidad. It's made by putting dents in the top of an oil drum and tuning them.

▼ **Metallophone**
The instrument you see here is from Bali. The bars are made of steel. The player strikes them with a mallet to make music.

Instruments that you pluck or strum

Zither. This folk instrument is still used in Europe.

Burmese harp. It has a long, curved neck. The strings are tuned with a silk thread that's attached to the neck.

Hawaiian mouth organ

Even with strings this instrument is held to the mouth to be played.

Balalaika. This Russian instrument has a body that is shaped like a triangle. It usually has three strings.

Samisen. This Japanese instrument is played by plucking the three strings with a flat piece of wood and ivory called a plectrum.

Instruments that you blow into

Panpipe. This instrument has been played for 2,000 years or more by people in many different parts of the world.

Alpenhorn. This horn is used by the cowherds in the Alps region. It makes a very loud noise.

Quena. This reed flute is a traditional Indian instrument from South America. The one you see here has decorations cut into the mouthpiece.

Ombiwe. This South African instrument is played by blowing into the round part at the top.

Eunuch flute. This instrument was made in Europe in the 17th and 18th Centuries. The player hummed into the holes in the onion-shaped cap.

- **To the Parent**

Many of the instruments that are now used only to produce music originally were used for ceremonial purposes and for signaling as drums and trumpets were. Musical instruments can be classified as they are here into wind, percussion and stringed instruments. Some, such as the piano, may be put into more than one category. The piano has strings, but they are struck by hammers to produce sound.

? Do Children Everywhere Start School at the Same Time?

ANSWER In many countries, including the United States, children begin school as summer turns into fall. But in other countries children start school at different times of year.

In Brazil the school year starts in February or March.

In Japan school starts in April, when the cherry blossoms are in bloom.

In elementary schools in Thailand classes start in May.

In the United States and Britain school starts in the fall.

In France girls and boys start the school year in September.

7 8 9 10 11 12

In Nigeria, too, the school year begins in September.

● To the Parent

In the United States and most Western countries the school year starts at the end of summer, usually in September. In the United Kingdom children can enroll in school when they are five years old, but to enable them to go to school as soon as possible enrollment is also open in January and April. The school year starts at other times of the year in countries such as Brazil and Thailand, depending on the region and on whether the school is public or private. In Japan people believe that April, when trees and plants start to bud, is the most suitable time to start school. The time when school starts is decided by a country's history and tradition.

? Does Everyone Celebrate New Year's?

ANSWER People in almost every country in the world celebrate the beginning of the new year. Their celebrations often include wishes or prayers for happiness and success in the coming year.

In China they set off lots of firecrackers at New Year's. They also eat fancy foods as part of their celebration.

In some European countries people like to dress up and enjoy a New Year's Day treat in a fancy restaurant.

In Cameroun and Nigeria, people form a circle and dance to the beat of a drum at New Year's.

In Australia New Year's comes in the summer, so people go to the beach.

In the United States people have parties to celebrate the coming of a new year. They gather in homes and other places on the night of December 31st. As the clock strikes midnight, they sing songs and congratulate one another.

In Japan people play traditional games and go to shrines and temples to pray.

● **To the Parent**

January 1 marks the beginning of a new year in Western countries and in many other parts of the world as well. In Japan the New Year's celebrations that begin January 1 are the most important holiday of the year. The Chinese New Year, on the lunar calendar, usually begins in February. The Jewish New Year begins with Rosh Hashana, which occurs in September or early October.

❓ Do Police Cars and Fire Trucks In All Countries Have Red Lights?

ANSWER In some countries the police cars have red lights on them, and in other countries they have blue lights. Another thing that's different from one country to another is the sound of police cars' sirens.

Peepo! Peepo! Peepo!

Wheo! Wheo! Wheo!

Pee Pee Pee

United States

France

Fire engines of the world

Canada
This truck is a pumper.

Germany
This is a fire engine.

United States. This pumper is yellow, but some are white. Pumpers spray water under pressure.

❓ Why Do People Use Animals To Do Heavy Work?

In snowy Arctic lands teams of huskies pull sleds loaded with people and supplies over great distances.

56

ANSWER All over the world, animals help people do work. They use animals because of their strength and ability to work long and hard. People choose animals that are suited to the land and climate.

■ Animals help by doing all sorts of work for people around the world

In India and other parts of Asia the elephant is used for carrying heavy objects such as logs and timber.

Horses are especially useful for pulling carts and wagons, and for carrying riders on their back.

All over Southeast Asia the plodding water buffalo is used for plowing paddy fields and dry fields as well.

Donkeys are very strong animals, which are used in many parts of the world to carry heavy loads of goods.

How Are Letters and Packages Sent to Other Countries?

ANSWER Letters and packages go the post office. If they are to leave the country, they are separated from the rest of the mail. Packages are inspected by a government officer. Then the mail is sorted according to where it is going. Finally it is sent on its way by boat, train or plane.

Letters and packages are sorted according to the countries they're addressed to. Then they're put on planes, ships and trains that carry them to where they are going. **4**

Packages that are going to other countries may be opened and checked by customs officials. **3**

2 You have to let the post office know what's inside a package that you want to send to another country.

AIR MAIL

1 Be sure you write the address clearly. If you want the letter or package to go by air mail be sure to mark it that way.

6

Packages and letters mailed from abroad are finally delivered to the people they're addressed to in just the same way that mail from the next town is.

When mail gets to the country it's going to it is checked by customs, then delivered.

● **To the Parent**

Because international mail involves two or more countries, its handling and carriage are governed by an international agreement. Not everything is covered by this agreement, however, and each country often decides independently on domestic delivery and other matters. In general the main difference from domestic mail is that parcels must pass through customs inspection. For this reason the contents of parcels must be declared, and if they are determined to be dangerous or perishable they will not be accepted for mailing.

World Mailboxes

Every country in the world has its own type of mailbox. The shape, size and color of a mailbox vary according to the country where it is found.

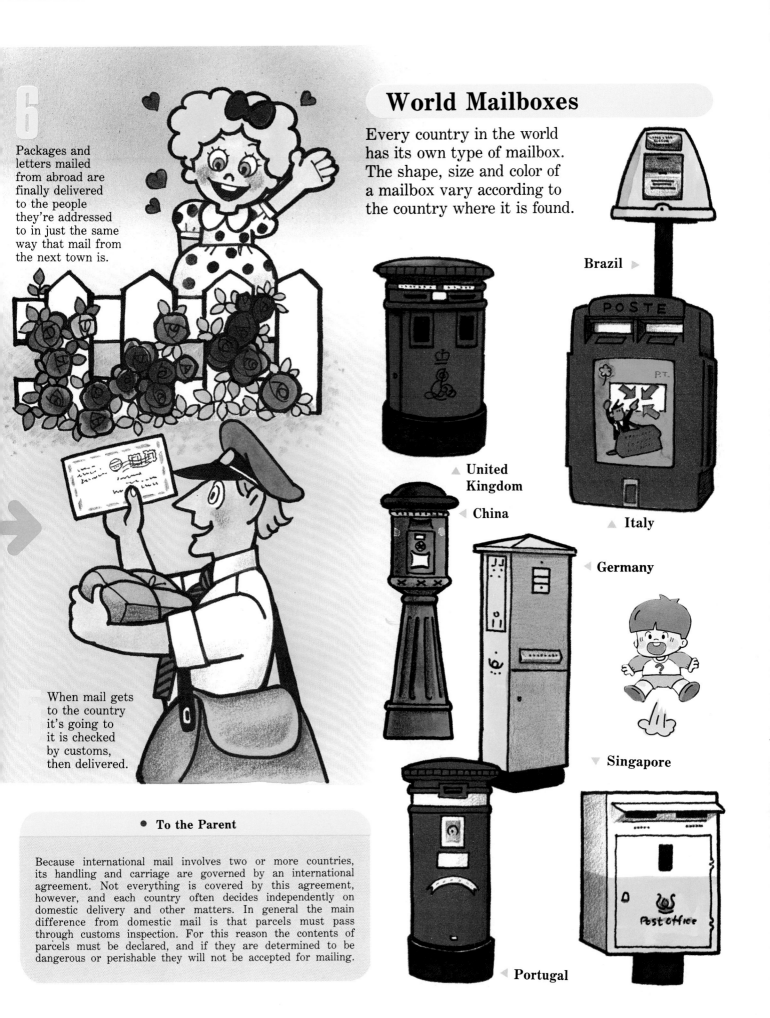

Brazil ▶

▲ United Kingdom

◀ China

▲ Italy

◀ Germany

◀ Portugal

▼ Singapore

59

Why Can We Talk by Phone To People in Faraway Lands?

ANSWER When you talk into a telephone your words are turned into electric signals. These signals can be sent to other countries by satellite or by cables that lie on the ocean floor. When they reach another country they are turned back into sounds like your voice and can be understood.

Telecommunication company

Earth station

Cable station

Telephone

Receiving a printed message

Satellite relay of TV

With a television camera, pictures must be turned into electric signals. These signals can then be sent all over the world. The signals are sent to a satellite and then on to other countries. This lets us see on our television sets what is happening in other countries.

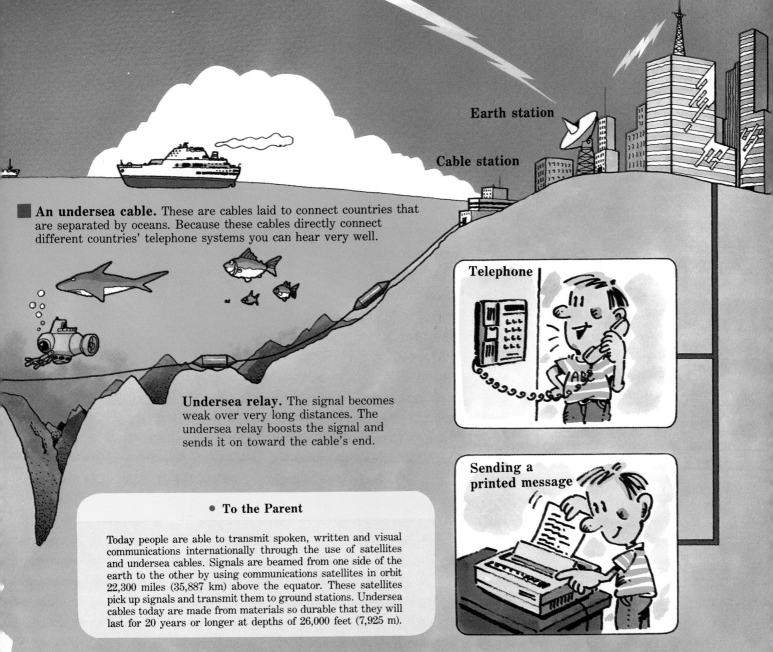

■ Communications satellites

These vehicles are put into stationary orbit, which keeps them in one place above the earth. They receive signals from one place on earth and relay them to other places. These signals go in a straight line. They cannot be sent along the ground because the earth curves, and the signals would go out into space. The satellites catch them and send them back.

Telecommunication company

Earth station

Cable station

■ An undersea cable. These are cables laid to connect countries that are separated by oceans. Because these cables directly connect different countries' telephone systems you can hear very well.

Undersea relay. The signal becomes weak over very long distances. The undersea relay boosts the signal and sends it on toward the cable's end.

Telephone

Sending a printed message

● **To the Parent**

Today people are able to transmit spoken, written and visual communications internationally through the use of satellites and undersea cables. Signals are beamed from one side of the earth to the other by using communications satellites in orbit 22,300 miles (35,887 km) above the equator. These satellites pick up signals and transmit them to ground stations. Undersea cables today are made from materials so durable that they will last for 20 years or longer at depths of 26,000 feet (7,925 m).

61

❓ Why Do Some People Remove Their Shoes When They Enter the House?

ANSWER In different countries people have different customs. In Japan people always remove their shoes before they enter a house. They wear only slippers and socks when they are inside. If you went to Japan for a visit you would have to do the same thing.

When Do Most Children Take Off Their Shoes?

In the United States and Europe children do not remove their shoes until the end of the day.

They eat with their shoes on.

They get up in the morning and put their shoes on.

In most countries children wear shoes in schools.

Even when they play indoors they hardly ever take their shoes off.

Why Do Some People Drive on the Left While Others Drive on the Right?

ANSWER Traffic rules change from country to country. In some places all cars, trucks and buses must stay to the right, while in others they must stay to the left. It all depends on the custom and law where you live.

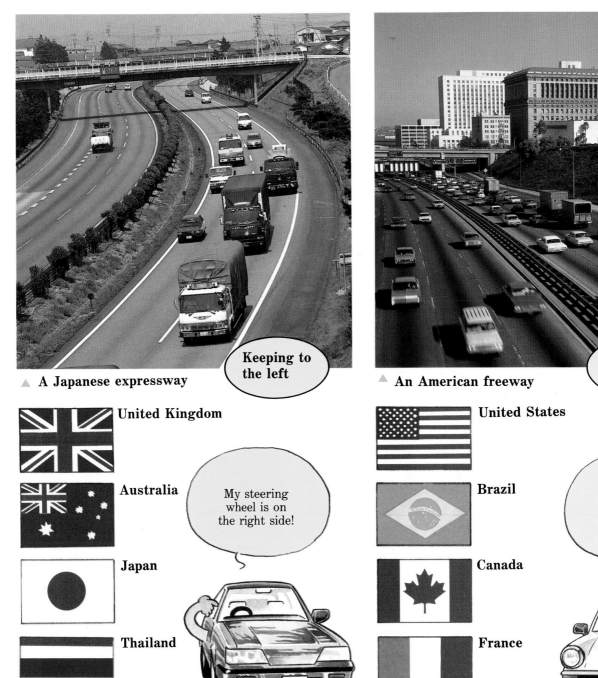

▲ A Japanese expressway

Keeping to the left

▲ An American freeway

Keeping to the right

United Kingdom

Australia

Japan

Thailand

My steering wheel is on the right side!

United States

Brazil

Canada

France

My steering wheel is on the left side!

■ Why England keeps left

Coach drivers in England sat at the right of the seat. But their whip might possibly have hit someone on the sidewalk, so coaches were ordered to drive on the left side of the road.

■ Why France keeps right

When the French rode in carriages the driver sat on the horse on the left. That made the horses pull to the left and step up onto the sidewalk, so traffic had to keep to the right.

The countries with the most cars

People all over the world use cars.
Large numbers of cars are manufactured in many different countries. Do you know which country has the most cars?

United States
168,607,000

Germany
27,071,000

Japan
44,524,000

Italy
22,833,000

France
24,110,000

❓ Why Are Costumes Worn on Halloween?

ANSWER Halloween is celebrated on October 31. It has traditionally meant that autumn is over. A long time ago people thought witches and evil spirits appeared on Halloween, so they put on costumes to hide from the demons. Today mostly children wear costumes. They collect candy or go to special Halloween parties.

On Halloween children ask for candy and other sweets. ▶

▼ Kids dress up in all kinds of strange costumes.

Fun and games

Many people hollow out the inside of a pumpkin, cut holes for eyes and a mouth and then put a candle inside to make a jack-o-lantern. They put the glowing pumpkin in front of their house.

Dunking for apples is a good Halloween game. Children try to bite into apples that are floating in a tub of water. They can't use their hands, so it is not easy to get hold of the apples. Everybody gets a very wet face.

● **To the Parent**

Halloween apparently began as an ancient Celtic festival to honor the god of death and welcome the winter and new year. It became fixed on All Hallows Eve, the day before the Christian festival of All Saints' Day, and has since been shortened to today's Halloween. It is now a time of fun for American children, and costume parties are held on this day, even at school. It is surprising that a day which represents death and the onslaught of a freezing winter has become a day for costume parties and fun.

67

Why Do Indians Bathe in a River?

ANSWER The people of India have great respect for the River Ganges. They believe it is the river of the gods of the Hindu religion. They also believe that the waters of this river have the power to wash away evil. Untold numbers of Indians bathe in the Ganges. Many people travel very long distances to bathe there.

▲ Indians bathe at Varanasi.

▲ They wash their bodies in the river.

The sacred River Ganges

Hindus believe that the Ganges will wash away evil and make their hearts pure.

■ India's many people

India has more people than any country in the world except China. More than 750 million people live in India. That is one and a half times as many as there are in all of Europe, even though India is much smaller than Europe.

People in India

750,000,000

Europe's population

500,000,000

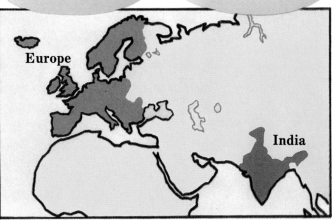

Europe

India

In India after some people die their ashes are thrown into the River Ganges. Hindus believe that the river's holy water will wash away their sins and that that will allow them to enter heaven.

● **To the Parent**

The River Ganges is sacred to Hindu believers. They believe that bathing in this river will absolve them of all sins and that committing their bones to its waters after death will assure them entry into heaven. At Varanasi, Hinduism's holiest place, more than one million pilgrims a year bathe in the Ganges. Pilgrims enter the waters from the bathing ghats, which are steps on the banks descending to the water. Women remain fully clothed and offer prayers as they enter the water. Men are often seen praying while seated cross-legged. Other ghats are known as burning ghats and are used for cremation of the dead. Their ashes are then committed to the river. Teach your child that there are many different religions in the world with different or unique customs and rituals.

How Did the Modern Olympics Begin?

ANSWER The credit goes to a Frenchman named Pierre de Coubertin. He knew that sport was a good way to bring people together. He proposed that the world hold a competition like they did in ancient Greece. That's how the modern Olympics got started.

▲ **Coubertin**

■ **The five rings**

The five-ring symbol was created in 1914 to recognize the five continents of the world that joined the games. The rings are locked together to show close and friendly relations among people of the world. This is the goal of the modern Olympics.

■ How the flame is carried

▲ Two women light the flame.

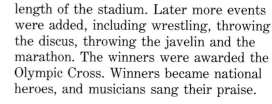

The sacred fire of the Olympic Games, which is lighted from the rays of the sun at Olympia in Greece, is carried by runners who relay it from one to another until it reaches the city in which the Olympics are to be held. To cross oceans the fire is transferred to a lantern and transported by plane or ship.

❓ What Events Did They Have in the Ancient Olympics?

The ancient Olympics began as an athletic contest held at Olympia in Greece in honor of Zeus, the king of the gods. In the beginning the games lasted only a day, and there was but one event: a footrace the length of the stadium. Later more events were added, including wrestling, throwing the discus, throwing the javelin and the marathon. The winners were awarded the Olympic Cross. Winners became national heroes, and musicians sang their praise.

Throwing the discus

Throwing the javelin

Wrestling

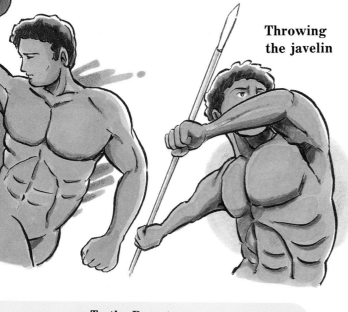

● **To the Parent**

The first Olympics are said to go back to 776 B.C., when athletic competitions were held at Olympia in Greece in honor of the god Zeus. Inspired by these ancient games Pierre de Coubertin believed that harmony among all nations could be achieved if the youth of the world were brought together in sports. He formed the International Olympic Committee in 1894 and held the first modern games in Athens in 1896.

How Did the Ancient Marathon Start?

ANSWER Many centuries ago the Greeks won a great battle against the armies of Persia at a place called Marathon. Marathon races began in memory of a Greek soldier who ran from Marathon to Athens to notify the Athenians of the victory of their mighty army.

The Battle of Marathon

News of victory

Why Isn't the Marathon Exactly 26 Miles Long?

The length of the marathon race is based on the distance the ancient runner covered from Marathon to Athens, about 24.8 miles (40 km). At first the exact distance of the race varied somewhat, and at the 4th Olympics in London in 1908 the distance was set at 26 miles and 385 yards. Since then that has become the standard marathon distance. Under the metric system the standard distance is 42.195 kilometers.

▲ Marathons for women are also popular in many countries.

The 1908 Olympics in London

Marathon rules

Like any other competition the marathon has certain rules, which must not be broken. Runners may not leave the set course, and they are not allowed to receive help from others during the race.

◀ Accept no help from others.

▼ Do not coach during the race.

▼ Don't leave the set course.

● **To the Parent**

The legendary Greek soldier's run in 490 B.C. was actually about 25 miles, but when the marathon was run at the London Olympics in 1908 the British Olympic Committee decided to start the race at Windsor Castle and have the finish line in front of the royal box in the stadium. That added the 385 yards, which has made the standard length of the race 26 miles 385 yards. The metric system measurement of 42.195 km is slightly less than a pace longer than that. Since marathon routes vary greatly in difficulty the International Amateur Athletic Federation does not recognize a record for the race.

Why Does February Have Only 28 Days?

(ANSWER) Our calendar was first used in ancient Rome. It was Emperor Augustus who decided that February should have only 28 days.

In the Rome of old, months with even numbers of days were believed to be unlucky.

Those with an odd number of days were thought to bring good luck.

Until that time the odd-numbered months (1st, 3rd, 5th, etc.) had 31 days, and the even-numbered months (4th, 6th, etc.) had 30 days. The 2nd month was specially devoted to the devil and therefore had only 29 days.

In English the eighth month is called August because in that month Augustus won a battle and gave the month his name. In those days even numbers were believed to bring bad luck, so he took a day from February, the second month, and added it to August to make 31 days, an odd number. The emperor just wanted to be very sure that his month would be a lucky one.

Now here's what I've decided to do. We'll take a day off February and add...

Let me see if I've got that right. He wanted to make a lucky month out of an unlucky one...

● **To the Parent**

In the Julian calendar established in 46 B.C. by Julius Caesar, odd-numbered months had 31 days and even-numbered months had 30 days. February, though, had 29 days in normal years and 30 in every fourth year, or what we now call leap year. Augustus, the adopted son of Julius and the first Roman emperor, named the eighth month after himself. But with 30 days it was unlucky. Augustus fixed that by taking a day from February and giving it to August. But now the emperor had created three consecutive 31-day months: July, August and September. That needed a remedy, and Augustus had it. At once he decreed that September-December must have 30, 31, 30 and 31 days.

Why Is It Easier to Swim in the Sea Than in a Pool?

ANSWER There is a lot of salt in sea water. Because saltwater is heavier than freshwater things float in it more easily. That's why it is easier to swim in the sea than it is in a pool.

TRY THIS

Make an egg float

1 Put an egg into a glass of water.

2 Add salt.

3 Stir gently and the egg will float to the surface.

 # Why Is It That You Can't Sink in Some Lakes?

Near Salt Lake City, Utah, is a very salty body of water called the Great Salt Lake. This lake contains so much salt that you can float easily in it.

● **To the Parent**

Saltwater is heavier than fresh and therefore makes objects float. The greater the concentration of salt in the water the greater the buoyancy will be. A swimmer can float better in saltwater and can therefore swim more easily due to this buoyancy. The Great Salt Lake in Utah and the Dead Sea in the Middle East are so salty that fish cannot live in them, and a swimmer cannot stay below the surface.

What Are These People Doing?

■ Guarding Buckingham Palace

The soldiers that guard Buckingham Palace in London wear decorative red uniforms and hats made of fur. When they march in close order on parade they look like the world's finest.

■ Picking coffee

Coffee is made from beans, which are the seeds of the coffee tree. The beans are picked by hand and then roasted. Today most coffee comes from South America, but it is also grown in Hawaii, Africa and other tropical areas.

■ Tapping rubber trees

The natural rubber that is used to make tires, balls and toys comes from the milky sap that is taken from the rubber tree. Many rubber trees are grown in Malaysia and Sri Lanka.

■ Picking cotton

The United States is one of the largest producers of cotton. It is still grown on large farms but is no longer picked by hand.

■ Harvesting wheat with a combine

In the United States farmers cultivate enormous fields of wheat using big machines such as the one you see here.

■ Shearing sheep

Large numbers of sheep are raised in Australia and New Zealand, and their wool is exported. The wool that is being cut off here using electric shears will be made into woolen cloth.

● **To the Parent**

At Buckingham Palace the traditional changing of the guard still takes place every morning. There are various kinds of industry and activity in different parts of the world. In many of these human labor has been replaced by machines. On large-scale farms or plantations the jobs of picking cotton and harvesting wheat are mechanized, making hand-picking and a horse and plow things of the past. Picking coffee beans and tapping rubber trees, on the other hand, are hard to mechanize and are still done largely by hand.

? And What Have We Here?

■ The Spanish flamenco

This woman is performing an exciting dance that is very popular in Spain. While a guitar plays she stamps her feet in a very dramatic fashion. Today people in many countries love to watch flamenco dancers.

■ Chinese t'ai chi

T'ai chi is a traditional Chinese system of disciplined physical training. It has recently gained popularity in the Western world as a technique for keeping the body in top condition.

■ The carnival in Rio de Janeiro

One of the most famous celebrations anywhere is held each year in this city in Brazil. People from all over the world go to Rio during the carnival and sing and dance for four days and three nights.

Growing-Up Album

What Country Is This Related To?

Various countries of the world have become known for certain unusual customs or activities which have often become cultural traditions. This picture shows customs or activities that we associate with different countries. Can you tell what country is related to each of the things shown?

1.
In this country many people wear a poncho over their shoulders and a wide-brimmed hat that is called a sombrero.

U.S.A.

Mexico

Netherlands

Britain

France

Spain

Brazil

2.
This country is famous for rodeos where cowboys try to ride wild horses for as long as they can without being thrown.

3.
Here coffee growing is an important industry.

4.
The flamenco, which is danced to guitar accompaniment, is a popular dance here.

5.
Windmills and tulips are famous here.

7.
The soldiers guarding
the Queen are famous.

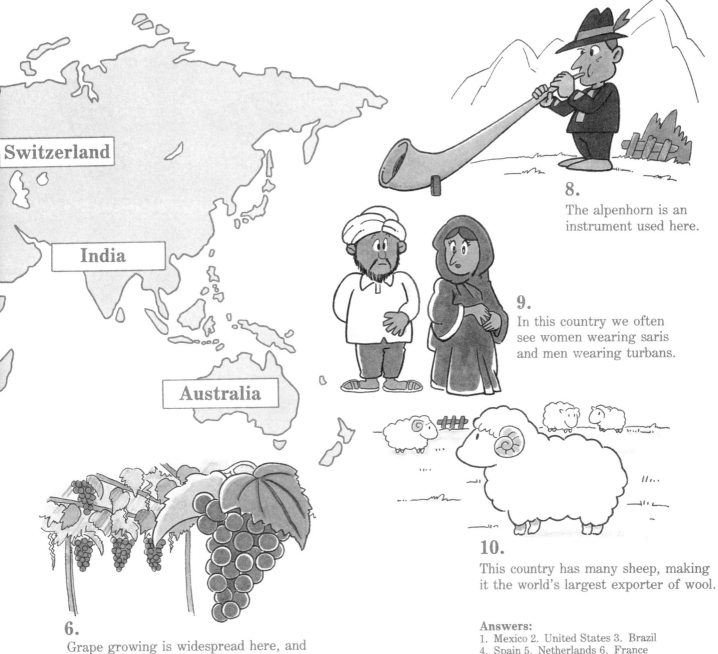

Switzerland

India

Australia

8.
The alpenhorn is an
instrument used here.

9.
In this country we often
see women wearing saris
and men wearing turbans.

6.
Grape growing is widespread here, and
this country's wines are very famous.

10.
This country has many sheep, making
it the world's largest exporter of wool.

Answers:
1. Mexico 2. United States 3. Brazil
4. Spain 5. Netherlands 6. France
7. United Kingdom 8. Switzerland
9. India 10. Australia

What Is the Correct Word to Use?

What word would you use if you were in the situations shown here? Take a close look at the picture before you answer and then try to imagine what you might say. Write your answer in the balloon beside the speaker.

The phone rings and you pick up the receiver.
What is the first thing you would say?

When you receive a gift what do you say?

In the morning what do you say to people?

When you bump into someone how do you apologize?

What do you say when you go to bed at night?

When you want to buy something in a store or restaurant what do you say to find out the price?

At a marriage ceremony what wishes do you give to the bride and groom?

What do you say if someone asks you the way and you don't know the right directions?

What do you say to your friends after school?

Have You Ever Eaten This?

Here we see foods eaten in various countries around the world. Look and see which ones you know, and place a check mark in the box opposite the ones you have actually eaten yourself. Do you know which country they come from?

Spicy hot curry

Spaghetti with meat sauce

A juicy sirloin steak

Fondue, pieces of bread dipped in melted cheese

☐ Paella, seafood cooked with rice

☐ A hamburger on a bun

☐ Cakes decorated with icing

☐ Roast stuffed chicken

☐ Delicious noodles in soup

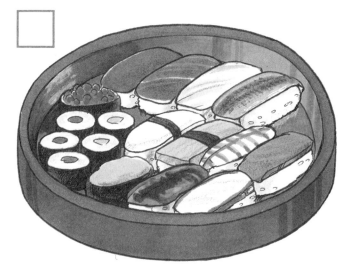
☐ Sushi, rice topped with seafood

A Child's First Library of Learning

The World We Live In

TIME
LIFE ®

Time-Life Books is a division of
Time Life Inc., a wholly owned
subsidiary of The Time Inc. Book Company
Time-Life Books, Alexandria, Virginia
Children's Publishing

Publisher:	Robert H. Smith
Managing Editor:	Neil Kagan
Associate Editor:	Jean Burke Crawford
Marketing Director:	Ruth P. Stevens
Promotion Director:	Kathleen B. Tresnak
Associate Promotion Director:	Jane B. Welihozkiy
Production Manager:	Prudence G. Harris
Editorial Consultants:	Jacqueline A. Ball
	Andrew Gutelle

Editorial Supervision by:
International Editorial Services Inc.
Tokyo, Japan

Editor:	C. E. Berry
Associate Editor:	Winston S. Priest
Translation:	Joseph Hlebica
	Bryan Harrell
Writer:	Pauline Bush
Editorial Staff:	Christine Alaimo
	Nobuko Abe

Library of Congress Cataloging in Publication Data
World we live in.
    p.   cm. — (A Child's first library of learning)
    Summary: Presents information, in a question and answer
format, about the customs, habits, and habitats of people from
different countries around the world with emphasis on what
makes their cultures unique.
    ISBN 0-8094-4885-8.   ISBN 0-8094-4886-6 (lib. bdg.)
    1. Manners and customs—Juvenile literature.
[1. Manners and customs.   2. Questions and answers.]
I. Time-Life Books.   II. Series.
QT85.W67 1989   390   89-20475
©1989 Time-Life Books Inc.
©1988 Gakken Co. Ltd.

Fourth printing 1993. Printed in U.S.A.
Published simultaneously in Canada.

TIME-LIFE is a trademark of Time Warner Inc. U.S.A.

Cover: *Magnum Photos/Eve Arnold*

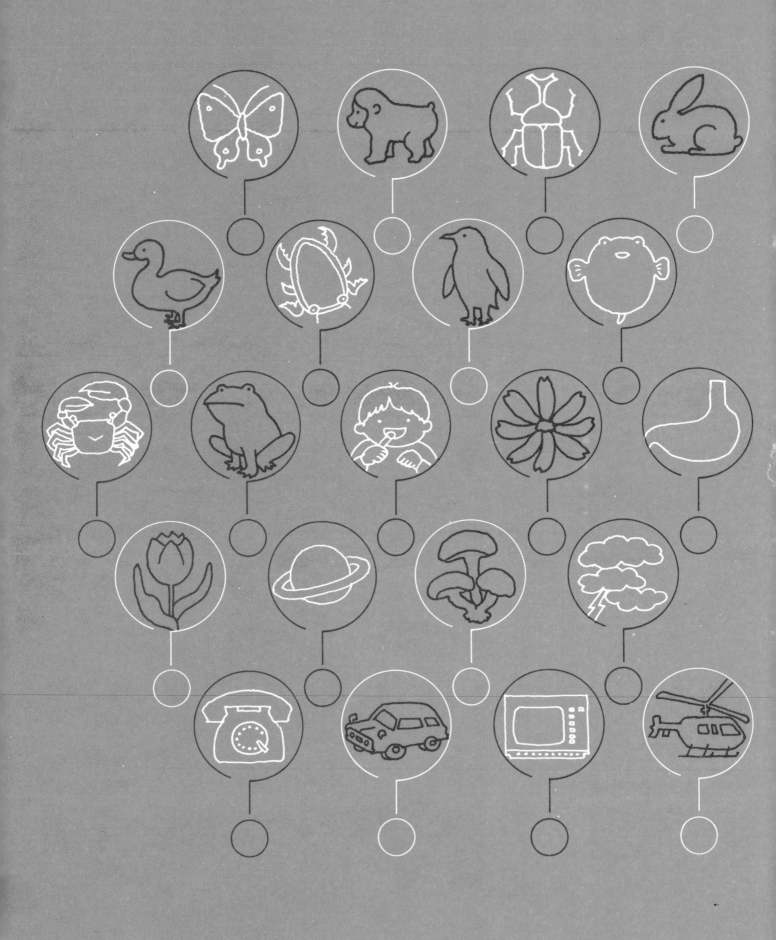